Motion

Debra J. Housel, M.S.Ed

Consultants

Sally Creel, Ed.D.
Curriculum Consultant

Leann Iacuone, M.A.T., NBCT, ATC
Riverside Unified School District

Image Credits: p.8 (top) NASA; p.12 akg/Johann Brandstetter/Newscom; pp8–9 dpa/picture-alliance/Newscom; pp.28–29 (illustrations) J.J. Rudisill; all other images from Shutterstock.

Library of Congress Cataloging-in-Publication Data

Housel, Debra J., author.
Motion / Debra J. Housel, M.S.Ed.
pages cm
Summary: "A scientist named Sir Isaac Newton wondered why things fall to the ground. He knew that forces made objects fall and move. Newton described three Laws of Motion to explain what happens when objects move."— Provided by publisher.
Audience: K to grade 3.
Includes index.
ISBN 978-1-4807-4607-7 (pbk.)
ISBN 978-1-4807-5074-6 (ebook)
1. Motion—Juvenile literature.
2. Force and energy—Juvenile literature. I. Title.
QC127.4.H68 2015
531.6—dc23

2014014114

Teacher Created Materials
5301 Oceanus Drive
Huntington Beach, CA 92649-1030
http://www.tcmpub.com

ISBN 978-1-4807-4607-7

Printed in Malaysia.
Thumbprints.45293

Table of Contents

Ready, Set, Move!

Everything is in motion. You see motion when you kick a ball. You feel motion when the wind blows your hair. You hear motion when a plane roars overhead.

Even Earth is in motion. It spins while it circles the sun.

This boy and the ball are both in motion.

Earth spins at around 1,000 miles per hour. That is about ten times faster than a car can go.

Motion makes the world go around. But sometimes, we need to stop the motion. We need the bus to stop so we can get on. Skydivers need parachutes to slow their falls. **Friction** and **drag** help things slow and stop.

Friction

Friction is a **force** that slows or stops motion. Without it, we could not walk. The ground would be too slippery.

Most moving objects slow gradually and then stop. Friction is a force that slows them. Think about roller skating. As you move your skates, the wheels press against the ground. The ground presses against the wheels. You must keep pushing to keep moving. If you stop, your skates will slow and then stop.

Whoa!

Snow has little friction. That is why we can easily glide across it on skis or a sled.

Drag

Things moving through air or water slow down, too. Drag is water or air **resistance** (ri-ZIS-tuhns) that works like friction. Drag is stronger in water than in air.

Shake It Up!

The moon has no air, so there is no air movement. Astronauts have to shake the flag to make it wave on the moon.

The faster an object moves, the more drag it has. People who design cars try to reduce drag. They shape the car's body so that air flows around it.

This car is being tested to see how air flows around it.

A force is a pull, push, or turn. Friction and drag are pulling forces. You move a shopping cart or pedal a bicycle by pushing. You open a jar by turning the lid.

There is no movement when forces are perfectly balanced. Have you ever played tug-of-war? If one team is stronger, that team wins. But if both teams are equal, the forces cancel each other. Neither team moves.

When forces don't balance, there is motion!

The horses pull the cart. They use force.

Sir Isaac Newton

Newton's Laws of Motion

Sir Isaac Newton was one of the world's greatest scientists. He lived in England long ago. He saw an apple fall from a tree. He wondered why apples always fall from trees. He thought about it a lot. He realized that gravity was the cause. Gravity is a force. It pulls all things toward one another. Large things pull harder than small things. Since Earth is huge, it pulls everything to the ground.

Newton figured out that gravity holds things in place. But it also plays an important role in motion.

Growing Up

Astronauts are a little taller in space than they are on Earth. Why? There is no gravity, so their bones move apart a little and relax.

Hockey players can hit a puck so hard that it may go more than 100 miles per hour!

The First Law

In 1687, Newton wrote a book. He wrote about the three laws of motion. The first is the law of **inertia** (in-UR-shuh). It says that if a thing is not moving, it will stay that way. It also says that if a thing is moving, it will keep moving in the same direction at the same speed.

If a force acts on a still object, it will move. If a force acts on a moving object, it will change its direction or speed.

The top will keep moving until a force makes it stop.

Laws

The laws of motion aren't like laws that police officers enforce. These laws are followed everywhere, by everything in the universe.

Think about a bowling ball on a shelf. It is at rest. Then, you pick up the ball and throw it down the lane. Now, it is in motion. When the ball hits the pins, it slows down. It may even change direction.

Inertia is not a force. It is a **property** that all things have. **Mass** is the amount of stuff something is made of. The more mass a thing has, the more inertia it has. Inertia is why you need less force to pick up an empty box than a full box.

The Second Law

The second law of motion states that a force can slow down, speed up, or change the direction a thing is moving in. You apply this rule daily. You choose how much force to use to pump a swing or hit a baseball.

This boy uses force to swing a bat.

When people play pool, they use a cue stick to hit the white ball. If they want the ball to cross the table, they use a lot of force. A larger force creates a larger change in motion. If they want the ball to go a short way, they just tap it with the cue stick.

This boy uses force to move a swing.

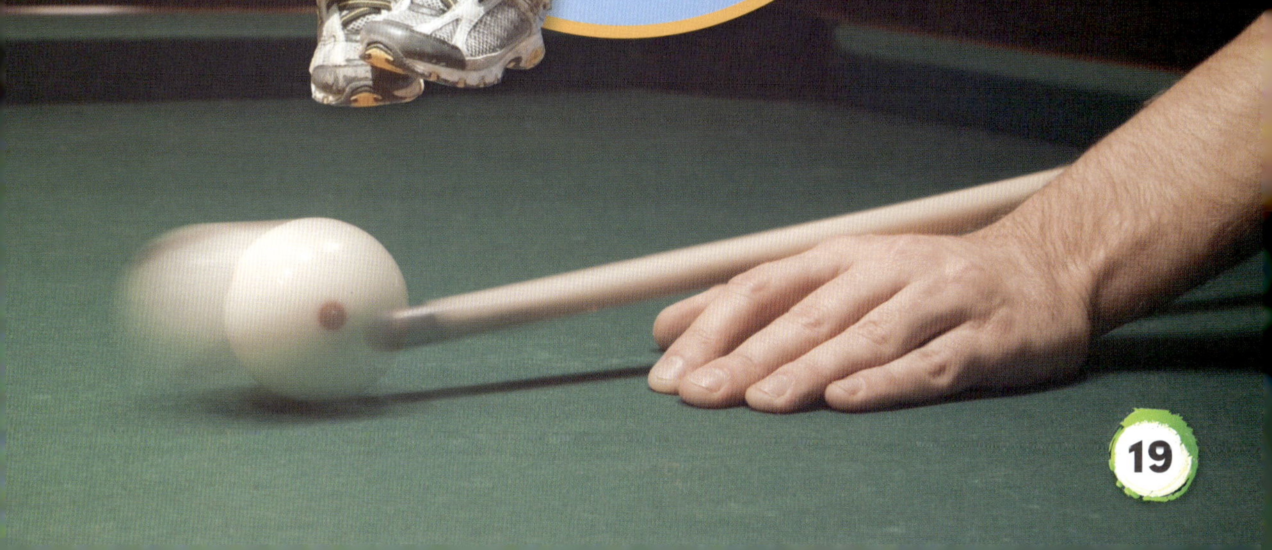

The Third Law

The third law of motion states that for every action, there is an equal and opposite **reaction**. Forces work in pairs. To take off from the ground, a plane uses the force of lift. Gravity pulls the plane toward the ground. Lift and gravity are opposing forces.

This plane uses lift to take off.

Tug-of-War

When you play tug-of-war, you feel the pull of the rope. The push of your feet against the ground is the equal and opposite reaction that keeps you from falling.

Describing Movement

Speed is how fast a thing moves. It is the distance something goes over time. Imagine you are in a car going 45 miles per hour. If nothing causes the car to slow down or speed up, it will go 45 miles in an hour.

Acceleration (ak-sel-uh-REY-shuhn) tells how much a thing's speed changes. As a car starts to move, you are pressed back into your seat. Once the car reaches a steady speed, this ends. You are not pressed into your seat anymore. When the car slows, your body still moves forward. It pushes against your seat belt. These are the effects of acceleration.

Acceleration and Mass

Acceleration is related to mass. A Ping-Pong ball rolls with just a finger flick. A basketball has more mass. To roll it at the same speed, you must push it with your whole hand.

Momentum is mass combined with speed. The more mass a thing has and the faster its speed, the more momentum it has. You can see momentum in action at a football game. One player tackles another. The player with the most momentum knocks the other one down.

The football player with the blue helmet has the most momentum.

Long Stop

A moving freight train has a lot of momentum. It cannot stop quickly. Once the engineer brakes, it may take a whole mile to stop!

The blue car's momentum was too strong. The blue car couldn't stop in time.

If you have seen a car after a crash, then you have seen the results of momentum. The car is crumpled where the **impact** occurred. If the crash involves a truck and a car, the car may have more damage. That is because it has less mass than the truck.

Motion may cause accidents. But the world would be dull without it. Nothing would ever move. You would not even exist! Your lungs must move to breathe. Your heart must pump blood. We need motion to live and grow. It is great to be in motion!

Let's Do Science!

What forces can you observe? See for yourself!

What to Get

- 1 hard-boiled egg
- timer or clock

What to Do

1 Gently spin the egg on its side. Observe its motion.

2 Gently spin the egg again. Use a timer or a clock to time how long it spins. Record the time on a chart like this one.

Spin Time	
Test 1	Test 2

3 Spin the egg a little faster. Time how long it spins. What happened? Think about how you spun the egg. How did this affect its motion?

Glossary

acceleration—the rate at which a moving thing's speed changes over time

drag—something that slows motion

force—a push, pull, or turn on an object

friction—a force that slows motion

impact—the act or force of one thing hitting another

inertia—a property of matter in which still objects stay at rest and moving objects keep moving at the same speed in the same direction

mass—the amount of matter (material) in something

momentum—the strength or force that something has when it is moving

property—a trait or characteristic of something

reaction—a force that opposes an action

resistance—a force that slows down a moving object

Index

Your Turn!

Paper Drop

Get two identical sheets of paper. Crumple one sheet into a ball. Stand on a chair or ladder and drop both papers at the same time. Does one hit the ground before the other? What force is at work?